FAMILY SYSTEM

THE COLORADO PRIZE FOR POETRY

Strike Anywhere, by Dean Young
selected by Charles Simic, 1995

Summer Mystagogia, by Bruce Beasley
selected by Charles Wright, 1996

The Thicket Daybreak, by Catherine Webster
selected by Jane Miller, 1997

Palma Cathedral, by Michael White
selected by Mark Strand, 1998

Popular Music, by Stephen Burt
selected by Jorie Graham, 1999

Design, by Sally Keith
selected by Allen Grossman, 2000

A Summer Evening, by Geoffrey Nutter
selected by Jorie Graham, 2001

Chemical Wedding, by Robyn Ewing
selected by Fanny Howe, 2002

Goldbeater's Skin, by G. C. Waldrep
selected by Donald Revell, 2003

Whethering, by Rusty Morrison
selected by Forrest Gander, 2004

Frayed escort, by Karen Garthe
selected by Cal Bedient, 2005

Carrier Wave, by Jaswinder Bolina
selected by Lyn Hejinian, 2006

Brenda Is in the Room and Other Poems,
by Craig Morgan Teicher
selected by Paul Hoover, 2007

One Sun Storm, by Endi Bogue Hartigan
selected by Martha Ronk, 2008

The Lesser Fields, by Rob Schlegel
selected by James Longenbach, 2009

Annulments, by Zach Savich
selected by Donald Revell, 2010

Scared Text, by Eric Baus
selected by Cole Swensen, 2011

Family System, by Jack Christian
selected by Elizabeth Willis, 2012

FAMILY SYSTEM

Jack Christian

The Center for Literary Publishing
Colorado State University

For information about permission to reproduce
selections from this book, write to
Permissions, Center for Literary Publishing,
9105 Campus Delivery, Department of English,
Colorado State University,
Fort Collins, Colorado 80523-9105.

Printed in the United States of America.

Library of Congress Cataloging-in-Publication Data

Christian, Jack, 1978-
  Family system / Jack Christian.
      p. cm. -- (Colorado Prize for Poetry)
  "Winner of the 2012 Colorado Prize for Poetry"--T.p. verso.
  Includes bibliographical references and index.
  Poems.
  ISBN 978-1-885635-27-3 (pbk. : alk. paper) -- ISBN 978-1-885635-28-0 (elec-
tronic)
  I. Title.

PS3603.H74567F36 2012
811'.6--dc23

                                        2012035442

The paper used in this book meets the minimum requirements of the
American National Standard for Information Sciences-Permanence of Paper
for Printed Library Materials, ANSI Z39.48-1984.
1 2 3 4 5   16 15 14 13 12

for Liane

CONTENTS

ONE

TWO

THREE

ONE

FAMILY SYSTEM

We're in a giant mom and dad linked by a heart.
We're going round in circles in the figure eight
made by their bodies and cinched by their heart.
Where their lips touch is another kind of heart.
Where their stomachs meet, a third type of heart.
They sort of know this, but they're too busy convulsing.
They think they're a constellation fastening in space.
And we're going with them on a vague run
for groceries. It's a long ride in a station wagon.
It's the screwy roads of an upper-class subdivision.
You think they resemble a galaxy spinning,
but to them you think it's like being inside two plants
joined at the stalk. Which might be right—
I've also been guessing. And wanting to twist
like they do, wanting to try some weird positions
and see what happens. I saw a model of it once:
A smaller arch passed under a bigger one
around what looked like a tomato slice stuck on a flywheel.
That's not how I'd describe it to them.

NEW REVISED STANDARD

A prayer is an edge with a bump in it.
String articulates a face; that's prayer.
Each prayer contains an I who traces a line
then stands on every point of it at once.
The Good is my sidewalk. When I'm tired
I link myself to a larger town
unsettled as of yet. My agitated arms grow knotted.
The term to describe this is *inextricable*.
It's paint mixed in water.
Its words often animals discussed across a grass.

A CIRCUMFERENCE

I want to walk the entire shore, around the continent.
When I reach a river
I'll have to decide whether to turn inland or go across.
If it's the Magdalena River
then questions and more questions.
If the river is yellow, then what is not so troubling in nature.
Where there's a hoop and hadn't been
and steam where I needn't any.
And where the world is bigger and my vision, too.
And in my travels a house droops to the bay
and a grove already into the bay.
A crank is spitting golden bits
and there are many geese. There are many kinds of birds:
ducks, large ducks, royal ducks,
ibises, egrets, herons, quail. I've seen falcons,
marsh hawks, sparrow hawks, goshawks and many other birds.

A TREE

What I was doing in the thunderstorm:
I was shaking my fist at the God of trash-talk.
I was stomping the footpath to the fencepost.
I parked—a star shot—I couldn't take it as coincidence.
I said a prayer to the God of sleeping outside
who's the same as the God of conniving.
I said a prayer for anyone who never came back.
I said a prayer to the God who answers back.
I said one for you if you chased your Gods away.
And one to the God of table manners
and to the God of horseshoes. And I said God
if you're God you're God of my lamplight
and of my undershirt. You're God of my feelings
which are mostly. But also of the trail I walk
but also toward a taller you.
Hey God, I finished the rock dam. I went in the field
and said one of patterned animal tracks and one to you
of cattle birth. I said one to the farmer Judy
who's always talking to herself
and one to the snapshot of the thing that's always happening.
I said God if there's the choice you're a God then
if everything's a choice.
This was in half-light in timber it was often.

MARIE

Karin's parents sent a couple nice wishes
and off they went around the bend on a Jonathan,
where the road can't Siobhan. Don was from Homer, Alaska—
Tuesday born, fathered by nonesuch, raised by Julia.
Graham did everything for a reason, was math proficient.
Nick did it for Eleanor. Aunt Jay did it with J.P.,
thereby upsetting many people. This made the newsletter.
Did you catch it? The guy we call "Japes." They printed it
"John Patrick." Marybeth conferenced with Lawson;
Angela copied Creech and cleared the changes through Jana.
Michelle told the boys to hit the presses. John threw his clothing.
Ryan flew to pasture. This meant Par 3 with Sterling,
executive ombuds. Andrew was impossible to locate.
Terence, like the dog will do. With Ray, there were goals,
which Ruth interpreted biblically. If she bore a child
she would name it Ruth. If it was a boy she would name its basket,
but still feel reprehensible. This was Saturday, Year of Manuals.
Jamie was to wed Alan then at the site decided by Mary Lyons,
who planned for violet; expected Meredith.
God Love Stonewall Jackson and Men of Vacation.
Tabitha reneged on account of charm school. Clay, gone to Maui.
Junior Chism, somewhat racist, still invited.
Cal was what Meg was bringing to the picnic. Sadie preferred "B-B-Q."
Garvey was modulated through potato salad.
There were "reasons." Put two "reasons" together,
they make a "foot." This, according to Jack's brother's thesis,

titled *Warren's Wonderful World of Made-Up Facts*—
not necessarily untrue. Thanks, Different Dave,
for pointing that out. Tulley is sorry to hear
of your arms and your legs. Nothing is impossible.
Last Bob saw, Jeffrey was starring in the movie
Boy of the Incongruous Response, or was that pertinent
only to Judy's online community? Liz was consoling the girl
the tennis team dubbed "Ice Boobs." What about The Flash?
What of Warm Roderick? All Mrs. Kent Collins wanted
was a word in the cube of the Poor Man's Seth Landman.
All Bill wanted were more curls. Saul told himself
he could tolerate the moniker "Fat Taco," so long as no one
said it to his brother. Rann was Israeli, besides. It wasn't a hoax.
The field had not released anything. This, with apologies
to Angela, who was starstruck. Peter's friends did and did not
resemble characters on sitcoms. They were and were not
scattered about the country. None were flyover people,
nor were they reincarnations, nor stories with beginnings, muddles,
and James, who was strangely present, Emma or not,
and accepted in that time and place. Vanessa.
They never began at his Wainwrights. They were Abigail,
clever as a promo. Kelly as Barbara. Her father, Talbot,
the lost pastor. Existed Mandy, photographer of record,
divorcée, the one the raft guide crooned toward.
Delilah was alive in the North. She called herself "Da"
when speaking with herself. Lucy's pet answered to "Tater Tots."

They bonded over mutual recognition of impermanence.
And Curt Evers was a basketball hero, from Appalachia,
usually excited. He was a fireball. Rebecca keyed piano well.
Melanie walked in the image of her mother Mamie Faye,
who carried a bundle of favorite things, known as memories.
And Scott was how Bonnie's Sue met a molecular Gary,
and Anne that Miss Dot was referred into the company
of Edmund Malone who was Darrell George and, for the most part,
Ronald Worthington.

MY LIFE

I had a nickname in that tribe I was an eldersomething.
I was the hardest name at the spelling bee.
I didn't sleep so much as start hallucinating.
My bathtub was claw-footed we weren't enemies.
Everything that was anything approached via animism.
Cars in those days were driven in through doorways.
The dark was a bottom I used it for traipsing.
If you were looking for me you asked by the boy of the land surveyor.
You gave the impression of the stranger
who drops in on Sunday school.
If it wasn't desert vacations it was New Jersey over Roanoke, Virginia.
I was a drinker of specific yolks and a causation
and an up-to-something.
The time I scammed 'em so bad they passed an ordinance about it.
In their Willie Nelson 1970s holding pattern.
So fat they lived in their own outskirts.
Occasionally, I got the feeling it was the feeling of neck-caught.
It was land zoned residential but in practice for chicken factories.
A jive I laid down I hoped the ties were tight enough.
Like a dust storm opposite the moon and no breeze at midnight.
I wished my vision was faster.
I threw my roses in the river.
The river took that hat away from me.

GLADETOWN CEMETERY

I took my car to it. It was covered in ivy.
There were deer. I saw a turtle.
The markers looked like motorcycle plates.
Some were poured of concrete.
The Ns and Ss were backwards.
I was talking to Phil about it. Right then,
on my cellphone. I saw a ghost in there.
I almost expected to. It was two feet tall and quiet.
It went between the graves.
It had a kind of business. I don't know what it was.
A skinny man. He pushed a small-wheeled carriage.
He was made of bluestone. His legs were long.
It was a skunk. I said to Phil, it's a dog
that started floating.
Or, how small off-leash dogs will glow.
It had a nest of cub-ghosts.
It started to disappear to places. It wanted out of there.
That's what was coming through to me.
This was at dusk. Exactly dusk.
The ghost shrank with the darkness.
I stepped in a mud puddle. I thought I'd go down Rt. 27.
Rt. 27 seemed like the best way home.

RURAL MANAGEMENT

I managed a grocery 40 minutes west of town. It was a warehouse. It was a place you could direct a letter toward. I had an office where I would read and my office was also full of food. On the outside, the bottom half of the building was painted. The top half was a natural white. When our shifts ended the staff and I would look back at it and consider it a thing that could be broken effectively. Then, the union came in and insisted: vests or aprons over blue jeans. "Or" was policy. They wrote it in the aisles in a script that approximated my handwriting. It was summer, and both parties moved in a direction of interconnectedness. The soup display was allowed also to occur in the dairy section. An ambiguity arose and through debate, I was permitted to drop a partner inside. I did so, and named her my cousin, Susan. With the market running so well, we coached each other in child-rearing because we were self-assured experts. She would say, "the cheese aisle," and I would find a manner in which "the cheese aisle" could repeat. She was sunburned. She sat long sessions on the curb waiting for her ride. Together, we pushed a shopping cart into the cattails at the edge of the lot. We pushed it on the half-path and on the footbridge across the Mill River. Ice clung in the eddies and the current curved the ice. It was bright out, and we were working through it.

I AM YOURS

And where we're here for supper tonight
and keep a thing of whiskey by the leg of the table,

and are nostalgic for the sense we have,
which is graffiti, and in circles around us.

This is how we like our nights and how we wind them.
Our nights are an arm-around. I cinch our nights closer to us.

They are first buds and branches' weight;
they are dark and enjoyable and to a bee.

Where we traverse the dam and its conundrum,
then replace it. Where a wind lifts at Heron's foot

and the wind goes through the night;
the night is no location. Nets cast because they exist

and we are where we walk, strong as cans,
extolled by night. I paint a boat to display the night

and take us to it. This piece is ours;
is no scheme of cognizance. It does not repeat.

ROSELAND

It's raining, but Matt says, that isn't rain.
You make tea with it
or it gets to you. It's an antelope.
In other converted basements the people speak Arawakan—
I'm just saying. Ours belonged to Harris;
we call it Harris's House.
His spirit wanders like the rest of us.
What we want is to stand in a breath.
Often, this is called the coffee sprout.
Some imply there is a blue rodent
but they are being Kafkaesque
and are drunk, or else enamored of the inarticulate.
We've four soups tonight, one with deer and shot in it.
With so many bowls I miss many people.
I picture them on the tips of a tree.
When the seasons change, they bring specialized knowledge
mysterious to the average person. Bishop and Leo,
Pablo and Tallulah are the names of their powers.
They are secrets of nature, alchemists in an original sense.
We're friends. We have fun.
At 5:45 we have an opinion.
I'm Daniel Schorr, we say.

A SIMILE

Certainty happens the way lovers persist in relation to sleep.
They search separate walks
in distant towns at the same hour of the night
when subtracted by their age difference.
One is dreaming. She tells herself a lie
in which she never rests. The other is wide awake.
He's determined as a list.
They find each other and think love is not unlike what it is to age.

A MIND IS MADE OF GRASSES

A mind throws itself in a lake and now it is an open pose.
And now it is a wooden frog.
In the snow nothing piles nothing moves.
The snow builds itself a covering.
Such is the way of it. This is a simile of the way.
And a step. And the way is spread over grasses.
And the clods get up and hustle.
The clods in front of everybody.

A GIANT REALM

We stood by the mill and told the stories of Fred, Ned, and Ed.
One time, Ned flipped a cement truck.
Ed owned a confident dog. Fred leased farm equipment.
Fred became obsessed with the unevenness of his face.

Ned said, God says cut-up in church.
Ed caught a fish with his hands. Ned didn't eat right.
The donkey nearly died when Fred fed it cake.
The donkey nearly broke my fingers when I saved its life.

A blue heron nested by the picnic area on the Upper Catawba.
Below the dam was the Lower Catawba. We moved to the mud.
The dog killed a muskrat. Fred climbed after pawpaws.

Ed found a bundle of wire in a stump by the bank.
Ned said, we could call up anybody.
When the blue heron landed it was because of our noise.

WIDESPREAD, PLAUSIBLE

We call it Total Animation.
We who are tracking an owl just now
and are knee-deep and speaking
of a thing to know of poplar trees
and of the pebble of trees.
And who do this of our overflowance
and despite misgiving, and whatever discomfort,
and whatever abrasion.
And we never see it. And are only about to—
held where a thing that never happens
hasn't yet. And whatever our making,
our heads are as if leaves burst from them in a day.

POEM OF MY HOPE

This month, Sarah is down and frequent in the backyard.
We make a point of eating together.
She's annoyed I called Connecticut
a dead sea-creature, mad I said her big cousin
is easier than making babies
and her children should be terrified
or else content to house their unknown hostility
until it localizes as stomach cancer.
What's crazy is how a family is its own school of painting,
how in mine the men carve the hedges
and the women carve their dresses
and when they get together their favorite color is skin.
It's obvious that these are white houses and those are white rocks
and there is the graveyard we enjoy
because it comforts us, because it hides death
but insists death is not hidden from us
and one day we'll lie around each other.
Sarah, you say you think about this. So then, consider me
in the act of bringing a thing over to you.
I'm waiting by the row that fronts our street,
where I'm sure this is the light we can practice with.
And that man in the next lot, he is our uncle, who grew tall,
and has stood for the decade since he gave up the church
and became the hoop at the end of the driveway.

TWO

A PARADOX

Although there aren't rules you are against them.
You bring curfew and we break it. You bring contraband
and strange light marks the sky, again.
Once, we were locked in the stem of a flower
that bloomed only at night. I was an owl who swooped low
before the car. You were the song you hummed.
We dressed in tassels and in leather. You made a map
from a barbed wire. You put on a shoe over a shoe over a shoe
and then you were a river, and then you were a bend.

IN A MEADOW ON A BEAM

at the end we would begin again
because there are instances wherein a notch
      is a wide-mile and a best-self
and could run-on-over or be folded in a backseat
        then covered in tied flies
           and later be a bowl but be *for you*
who resemble a spot of sun and also a motion
       whose motion is over-there
like to the victor go the things we jinx by talking about
      and then they happen anyway
out where we pushed all the weeds down
and where the weather approaches aesthetic necessity
      and our reason with no holes
         floats seven feet down the creek
that's when our awe reveals itself
and comes full-on in a ghost-step

MORE LIKE A FACTORY

My great-grandfather was all short-circuited
when he took off his crash helmet. He loved needling

more than anything. He did it at a discount. He was a man
of many ropetricks, in the habit of a dust collection.

He believed in bringing a boxing glove. He said he'd do without
the other shoelace, was fine without utensils. His inheritance

was engine oil. This sentiment skipped a generation.
He drank like his mother. It took her six nips to fly,

eight years to drive stick shift. What she wanted most
was to be good-for-nothing. She sat you down and told you so.

Her brother had a mallet fist. Her father was a flour sack.
Before him, a deckhand, a feather-head. Before then,

nobody knows. But still, a family. She had three aunts. It's true;
they passed off into different languages—their river

with no blood, their canopy sun and their arms the poles
to hold it up. The older two chickened out, but the third

went on and on. She was insistent. She was a chant. Her words
came down through penny wire. Her husband said her star

petered out. It wasn't like a bomb went off. She was never
quite his. She wasn't exactly anybody. He couldn't remember

if he wanted her or not. He coughed up a manual.
He coughed up a hex nut. He kept his distance

under a padlock. We keep her fingers album-pressed.
We keep a room of him, a fourth stomach, an iron cup.

REPORTER

When I said the place was *square,* I meant *and dusty.* When I met its inhabitants, I lost my cool, tried to copy their country mannerisms. I wrote about it, but their voices were not in my head. Though it was for their sonorous, crooked chirping that I believed.

The man among them cowered in corners and also, too, had a shadow-him that was an animal and a weed, and who sometimes left a sawdust trail no one could follow. Except in a car. His fingers made screws I thought were letters impossible, and so told him, incessantly, until I assumed his shadow-him was a shadow-me—I, I mean. And the phrases between us became unbecoming.

His pair of sisters kept an eye toward what all they could encounter. In front of their gaze I continually confirmed the things I thought I wouldn't; and when they told me of their ways, I too believed and was immediately aligned with my five or six shadow-selves, minus rib-fat and, one time, shoes.

The memory of them recurs. Makes me drive too fast and sing too loud and eat their music, which isn't anything at all—an inward yawp that sounds only for those, like me, who fled with their windows wide, who prickled in its irregular breeze. But when it hits, I hear the question phrased thusly: Do I want to save the changes?

AFTER A PAINTING BY HENRYK FANTAZOS

The Swampwater Baptism includes a gator as expected
and a man who rides the gator, which is permitted,
and a gown that gets wet, but not exclusively.
Then, there is another gator, and a woman who kicks
and pilgrims by her sides. There is a preacher in pink—
the good are wearing white, the people are wearing white—
and a drawing on the water, then sketch marks on the water
and a harpoon from out of nowhere, from the sky
if someone thought of it. The harpoon totes a line
the color of a creeping plant. Also, there is mud
beneath the water. There are church suits, outdoor hats,
suspenders, swamp boots and hidden shoes. The trees grow
not on the banks but in the shallows and grow plumb,
taking growth literally. There are stumps that were never trees
and roots without their trees and roots beneath.
Centrally, there is a bible. There are nameless bits afloat
and the light is nameless. It is blue but pale.
Elsewhere, it diffuses yellow or is indistinguishable
from red bushes, branchless, allotted their leaves.
All this behind the water, the form of its backdrop,
the landscape's fact in the case someone believed it.
The water is the Haw River, spilt over low banks
before the curve at Raven Rock.

A FENCE

The knowledge that our field had no end made us wild to suppose one. Doing so, we started to poke around, cleverly, to see if anything had changed under the weight of our new thought. Sure enough, a wall had grown way out in the distance. The sun had already found it and was beaming down upon it. That, and our feet were a little bigger.

Already, a band of boys was running toward the wall. They were wrestling each other to see who would be first to climb it. And, when several succeeded in crossing over and back, they returned to the rest of us just as quickly.

In garbled language, they told of strange, hooded people they'd seen. They said when they announced themselves to these people, the strangers stopped what they were doing and said simple words like "Hi," "Fine," "Thanks." Some of the more gregarious of them even engaged the boys in talk about the weather, which was perfectly nice.

One of us asked, was there any hostility or confrontation? All the boys said there wasn't. But none could explain why his mouth was full of rocks.

RESPONSIBILITY

The weather's canned today.
It's done this before.
I feel cheap when I applaud it,
but sometimes the weather needs us
to say it's OK if the sky gives out,
if it goes home early and we stay inside.
Last night, my one leg grew longer.
I had a moment in a hot air balloon.
You were there, but not happy about it.
You went up anyway, so thanks.
This morning sprung a new theory of gray.
The city came by for the trash.
I found a science of imaginary solutions,
which was a good thing:
The car had a flat. The kitchen was bombed with dishes.
Our dog was lost but he was returning.

EIGHT MONKS IN UNISON

This is the myth of retrospective cohesion.
My friend Mike tends to take the idea in a high-five direction.
He lies on the floor, considering basketball.
He wants to say, "The snow's green out there."
He says it. The snow is white and the grass is green
and the sun is shining. There's one cloud so particular
we want it to stay with us. It moves closer to Agawam.
We don't go anywhere.
Now Rachel comes over and presses herself to the back of me.
We decide the road looks like a nomadic leaf sculptor
went walking up it and down it. That his life's work took a day.
There's an apple in the mailbox.
In my Shojutsu ink drawing, a man turns to another man
who turns to another man
and they do portraits of one another.
This is called concatenation.
This is called "Self-Portrait in a Conventional Setting."
Mike, it was like, "Time to stencil your likeness
on my passenger-side window."
It was like an important outing or date
might find us early to eat Thanksgiving pie.
Rachel, while we were doing our good neck exercises,
I took a picture of us.
The area rug and apartment made a new room together.

MARCH WITH WOUNDED HOUND

In the circle I made the dog move
        made pear trees move
And this was good to me if it was
If a piling-on if a pear tree
If all else well spring to you
A ritual walk then a spring ritual
        a circle to anybody
            and a tail to you and a dog
Wisteria and twila and an airplane
Then an airplane then a palm frond
My ritual was azaleas bloomed
        crocus bloomed
Good Tuesday and all to anybody
Or more than anything something pear
        made of dog then of scenery

ORGANIZATION IS ALSO A MAKING

All image is impossible. The road personified
becomes the night. When archers gather in the city
they are husks of seed, their stillness only a symbol,
and the deep world is a lie. Our moss steps
and our hid-song, too. The circle drawn of necessity,
and at the gesture's heart a sound to imagine.
The river joins the ocean but not to change it.

AS SURELY

Our clothes were only blankets.
Our tunes were of motorboats
were of thoughts gone on.
In our powwow of laundry and ornament.
In our smack talk and in our nearness.
With our owls of daybreak their calls the same.
This was our anterior house
where faith. We had a fish not caught right.
And a picnic implement. And a recess
where efficiency. And an engine we tended.
On a spool and on a line.
This was our coincidence.
We were elbow-bent. And held tight around
and toward. And in or rather in response.
Straight through the plum of our hearts.
And in our quickness and in what goes up.

A HILL

Virginians remember Virginia was the threshold of a giant realm
which was a table.
Around it, friends smiled, got weird, got married.
Friends held bouquets. They brought their hogs and donkeys.
Some built houses. Some dressed in period garb.
Some shot each other.
Some lay on the table and practiced the dying method.
That was one method.
Another was applause. A third was movement.
A fourth was buds on branches. A fifth was a line of sight
and a fence post, and humidity.
A sixth was coming back.
When they came back, their roads were stumps. Their rooms were odd.
They travelled Interstate 81 of compulsion
and there was no heaven.
Heaven was a thing to be big-hearted about.
Its untruth was also good.
They considered the banal. They considered a blue heron.
Around the table, they were memorable and grand.
They tried to walk to Chicago.

A CATARACT

A Public is a vehicle by which we are transported,
Jack and I, of the racer set,
who in our vision happen rapidly
because we're construed of rocketpack.
And while we're glad
our land is pocked of stone and houses,
our air is more a branch. We hold it by its end
and we mean it to persist as an invitation
and we hope it does make appearance as a trail to you.

LET'S COLLABORATE

Over mud, I walk the plank toward God
who got up again recently, and I rose early to meet him.
Check out this dream: There was Jesus,
only he was just that long-haired kid
who lives down the street and is always smoking cigarettes
beside my porch and it was me who woke him up
who bailed him out, because his alarm
had been going off for hours.
I was pretty nice. I said, "Hey, Dude. Get up, it's Easter."
The daffodils survived the freeze.
The Mexican kids were in the alley crushing pink eggs
with a soccer ball and a bike.
They were crazy with palm fronds.
I was kind of still asleep, and you know,
talking like my people who come from the country.
I said my favorite place is a road in Virginia
at a certain speed so when I swerve
over the rise at Chancellorsville I don't lose it on the battlefields.
All I see are placards and shrubs. And if I make it,
I start to sing whatever's on the radio.
And when the road bends like the general's arm
and shoots me straight through the valley's heart,
there's a kid humming "Loving Nancy" in the ditch
and the stuff on my face is as much blood as it is dust.
And suddenly, it's the warm glowing night

I thought we could all ride into together one day.
The sky's vacant like an airbrushed painting,
like a Super-Sargasso Sea, where what's lost
has the responsibility to pop back up again.
Given the apartment theory of dimensions
we could say, "Fuck it," or we could gather the proof
necessary to believe in everything no one can see.

THREE

HELL IS FIRE HEAVEN IS CAKE

In a yard of hollow trees
I could hear the echoes of smitten children.
I could hear their birdsong imitation.
I was wrapped up in a fraying blanket.
I was holstering a bad revolver.
I was adding cement to a pillow fort.
It was hard to see with the money over my eyes.
I had a spray can of paint and I was
hot on the trail of a bushwhacking tractor.
On my chest I wore a plastic star.
I'd set up camp on the cattle grate.
I was eulogizing a squirrel in a shoebox.
I was being lowered down in a pine box.
I was flying a balsawood airplane.
My mission was to gather the fog
that still hung between the rises in the meadow.
No one could see me in the magnolia.
I floated out on the silver water.
I shimmied up a yellow rope.
I did the snake dance for Saint Peter.
In the side mud, I lost my sandals.
I chose from a variety of cobweb dresses
in a gigantic forest. It was okay with me
to tend the fire inside the mountain forever.
Or, I was ready to eat dessert, after dessert, after dessert.
But I wanted to know how my friend Marc Kuykendall went.

MOURNING PICTURE

The sheep is cracked and the girl is not.
The still girl tends a sad sheep.
A ribboned bonnet lies patient on the ground.
The dandelions are up. The boxelder alive
nevertheless. The shrubs warm and ample.
A doll looks toward the ridge beyond the yard
where light remains and the stonework is cracked.
The ridge is loving in descent.
In their summer chairs and mourning clothes,
the parents gaze across each other. Their girl wears stripes.
The farm cat stalls, approaching.

YOU'RE RIGHT I DID ENJOY THE EXCURSION TO THE BUNGALOW

and the experience of the daffodil
where the waterfall was what a surprise
and the road we wanted was the road we were on
      by a different name so we made it
where the fire pit and the fire the stars and both of us
      and our amazement and the branch we didn't burn
the yard art in the wild manicured lawn
      the kindling the string of lights
            our marshmallow sandwiches
and what we carved and the child from whom
      we hid the chocolate
the shorted porch light and the stones
      where we stooped and dozed
how we'd be with the split logs in wait
      the beer undrunk the low-percentage chance of rain

TWELVE SONGS

In cycles, I replace the term *father* with *Neil Diamond*.
I do it at Easter, traipsing through woods and meadows.
I have an image of him lost in a parking lot,
wearing a crash helmet and short sleeves,
finding a particular storefront newly vacant
and marking this in his posture.
He visits planetariums, eats hot dogs.
His process is of leaving.
He turns a key. He loops a hand behind a passenger's back.
He doesn't know the transformation that places him
beneath lights in a studded suit, where he plays
and is at-play. When he sings, intensity is meaning,
and in this there is rebirth and also absence,
a paternal kind, e.g., the distance between stadiums,
and the black where the audience hunts, correctly,
for a sure, dumb earnestness, his clenched hand and wide stare.

AN APE

I walk a dog-colored thought to the All Dog Chapel
of Lost Dog Souls
where I purchase a translucent retriever.
Though I gather he comes without a name
I know to call him Bounder.
I feel this strange fire. A statue leaps through itself
on the courthouse promontory. A slow-moving humaffalo
crosses the street. My hands are indulged by palsy.
There's a bawl I make
when I can think of nothing but warm laundry.
I think this is a sort of salvation.
I walk through a more forgotten afternoon
proceeded by similar, later afternoons.
A fold of infants is shepherded by me—are guarded by my mouth.
I arrange my bones in a pleasing figure
so that I might fall to sleep inside them.

TAXONOMY

In the yard a tarn is growing,
is defining itself by parts of itself.

That is what we call chance
and plot its progressions on a board

and say what flies are Purple Martins
and nothing is a condition of the magnolia.

Nothing is floating inside a jar.
We can place it. Then, we hold it close.

We push it against the door.

So how a bug? So how this martin frozen
and this one bubbled-up, and these make one bird and go?

OUR AIR IS MORE A BRANCH

I know if we sit together long enough
I'm going to put my arm around you. We're going to lose time.
We'll be surprised, later, when the day has changed,
that it was ordered and now is not,
and we were going a great distance
but it was always just another rise
on the vague path that follows the ridge.
You can see where to go by the patterns of branches
and by looking up where it's still a little light
and by picking your knees up
and making your feet more sure than the rocks and roots,
by the one star that traces from west to east
because it's a satellite,
and sureness is a thing to tell about.
There's the fairgrounds, and the airport,
then the cornfield approaching the river.
The river is hidden by a row of trees.
Some days I climb to vantage points and look out at places
and imagine myself there.
If I walk too far will you pick me up at the top?
There's an abandoned house and a place to park.
If it storms I'll sit on the bench on the covered veranda.
The view is the kind I want to see how far
a paper airplane would sail—but it wouldn't go far—
and where I see the hills are older than the river.
I went up enough I could name all the peaks

from the helpful diagram.
I named them all after people who'd died,
then later, renamed them, in spring when I had that much energy,
and again on a snow hike and lost taking pictures.
We can find my car on our way back
from a dinner somewhere else.
We'll see the discovery as part of the pleasure
that one thing leads to another,
how it's socks then shoes, then from the house and back,
and goodbye-for-real, and the day is next.
The evening is after that.
There's a baseball game.
There's a pitch in baseball that is fast as hell,
and is more notable for being completely accurate,
and actually has no velocity.
With a pitch like that, it's true, there are a million different things
to think for a second to hurry after, but don't.

WE'RE CHANGING IRONY

We're changing our heads to mean *slightly off*.
When we stand, we struggle with our knees
because the fuzz has filleted the equilibrium in our eyes
which, did we mention, are slightly out.
We're counting with our fingers that are grossly out.
We're thinking in our temples, which means
bad news for gaffes.
We're clapping with our feet that are mostly crunched.
And in our treehouse, well, there are some secret rituals.
And in our fortress, we're shooing the poetasters out.
We're pleading with our fabrications that are highly miffed.
We're talking Paul Bunyan in our voices
(but when a larynx goes to chirping
we remember to spit the tadpoles out).
When the designer sends frowns
we loom in rain we've tuned to melt.
We're pending in a motion that is tacitly illicit.
The tenacity in our torsos is what we deserve
for being so frank.
We're caterwauling in the wind while our children pout.
We're grouping our hounds and making sweet music
with flashlights, and nobody's shocked.
We've sharpened our followers.
We've killed our socks.

EARLY SPRING

The yellow-spotted salamanders have crossed Henry Street
and in buckets been taken across
by glad people who stand in rain and fog near their houses
then stand in nightshirts before their beds
then dream of where the wilderness gives way to its towns
and how towns bend back to countrysides.
For all of these their way is to bloom.
For instance, where the water catches the light
then drops from a rail in the spring's first thunderstorm.
Then, where water discards the light,
and the crocus up earlier this year.
A miracle is at once to carry and be carried.
Belief is a common-book of travel.
There are many of us, then the prints that go before us join,
then the dark changes color, and on the edge of the forest
a gray bear unfolds itself.

NORTHAMPTON ECSTATIC

When great movies are in my device which is clean
and I'm on my couch got secondhand
with elderberries in the compost and fruitflies in the kitchen
Chickens I'm to meet in weather unapproachable
and the river I unhinge
Gift bags full with lemonade powder
in time for reenactment
And often on the perimeter of thought on a knotted street
The governor necessary to incite these things:
the calm, the golfcart and ugly shrubs
the way unrumored but repeated
A prayer for courage
which is superior to the feeling of being brave
and is brought by our bumblebee, our mother's rose
her dogs who mistake swimming humans for boats
and attempt to climb aboard
A caterwaul across gravel
Mom's quilt in the graveyard
The light the bricks take
The brick and ivy together
Our great speckled bird by exhortation—
how sane to be a knucklehead with a wagon to tote a friend in
across the bridge with the traffic jam
The sunspot on the sidewalk travelling near to me

ANOTHER EDEN

Serendipity, we had it.
We weren't looking and there it was.
The river snuck up on us.
The river was always paddling.
We were glad to see each other,
so glad we lost the canoe.
That didn't make a bit of difference to us
because we were making love.
After that, we were eating squirrel.
We wanted the birds to give us something.
They gave us a load of crap.
We had to laugh about it.
We had to dig in our bellies
and get our laughs. Then,
we listened for the raccoons to shriek.
Then, we remembered The Woods, silently.
It brushed my shoulder once
when I bent to loose my shoe.
It's kind of funny what we did out there
with the fire in our eyes.
We called putting our arms
around each other canoodling.
When we were bored, we dressed like fish.
When we tired, we washed up on the banks.
We had to laugh about it.
We had to keep thinking of all the other places
we could try and not find.

GOTHIC PEOPLES INSTITUTE

And were you cold last night
and in dreams somewhat amphibian.
Was it sometimes a coldfront. What do the gestures mean
if they aren't the same as other gestures.
What when their hands have gotten past each other.
Has this one started a hiccup. Has he ridden a four-wheeler
or, were the apples imported maybe. Did the leaves change more
or again. And was the creek turned by hoofprints.
If this was an inside what would it look like.
If they rubbed here would they prize vision so much.
If not, where to swim to. Where to go round again.
How to paddle there. Is it a bog. What do you suggest.
What if you washed up. What if she aged years in seconds.
What makes him cringe then. What causes laughing fits
and have you practiced. And were they mountains.
Is that Monadnock and Seven Sisters there. Did the preparation
mature them well. Were they worn. Were they pants.
What found he was fossilized. And did it wrinkle him.
Did the things he said resemble sculpted stone.
What about a woodcut. How about an airplane
with a lawnmower on its wing. How about that.
If a thing is loved enough, does it equally experience time lapse.
And when does love get lied to. When appropriate
for singing about. Does it build in the manner you accumulate.
Is it held by vacancy and noticeably troubled by it.
Would they prefer another choice. Which, on a nametag.

What about a tar patch. Which keeps one later. Which more easily
taken for confidence. Which for anarchy. What about
an uppermost part. What about on a roadtrip.
What, for the sake of confusion.
And do your feet turn in the shape of hallelujah.
Do the prayers travel well. Are they like fruitcake.
In any case, how do they meander. Or, is it we'd better fling them.
Are those insightful to hear about or just kind of
some private thoughts. Like noodles then. Discernable in darkness maybe.
How hokey do we become. And how many do we commemorate.
Did she bring-it-on then. And those by circumlocution then.
Or, gathered otherwise. Can you draw it. Can he drive it.
Was it seen like our own hand. And how was the ceremony.
Did society-folk attend. Did moons rise in storefronts.
Were they a club with membership dwindling.
Could any of it be danced to. Would it describe as seasonal.
Would it present standardly. Were they a bird's nest.
Was it a church-on-wheels.

ACKNOWLEDGMENTS

I am grateful to the publications where the following poems first appeared, sometimes in different forms:

Sprung Formal: "A Tree," "A Giant Realm"
Sixth Finch: "A Mind Is Made of Grasses," "I Am Yours," "A Cataract"
Web Conjunctions: "Widespread, Plausible," "March with Wounded Hound,"
    "In a Meadow on a Beam," "Gothic Peoples Institute"
Denver Quarterly: "A Circumference"
Ink Node weekly feature: "Roseland"
Diagram: "Family System"
Drunken Boat: "New Revised Standard," "Eight Monks in Unison"
Notnostrums: "Marie," "Rural Management," "A Paradox"
Meridian: "Hell Is Fire Heaven Is Cake"
Mississippi Review: "A Fence," "Reporter"
Invisible Ear: "Let's Collaborate," "An Ape"
Cimarron Review: "Poem of My Hope," "Gladetown Cemetery"
Noö Journal: "My Life"
Phoebe: "As Surely"
H_NGM_N: "You're Right I Did Enjoy the Excursion to the Bungalow"
751 Magazine: "Responsibility"
Jubilat: "We're Changing Irony"
The Hat: "A Hill" "More Like a Factory"

Some of these poems appeared in a chapbook, *Let's Collaborate,* published in 2009 by Magic Helicopter Press in a print run of seventy-five copies.

Many thanks to David Bartone, Jenn Blair, Luke Bloomfield, Karin Bolender, Steven Byrd, Francesca Chabrier, Chris Cheney, Bill Christian, Melinda Christian, Warren Christian, Sam Cross, Christy Crutchfield, RHW Dillard, Gabe Durham, Jessica Fjeld, Brian Foley, Noah Gershman, Peter Gizzi, Rachel Glaser, Stephanie G'Schwind, Cathryn Hankla, Henry Hart, Julia Hauser, James Haug, Hutch Hill, Ben Kopel, Marc Kuykendall, Lily Ladewig, Mark Leidner, Richard Lucyshyn, Liane Malinowski, Phil Pinch, Lisa Radcliff, Jon Rovner, Tomaž Šalamun, Zach Savich, Nancy Schoenberger, Sylvia Snape, James Tate, Emma Terry, Chris Tharp, Sara Toombs, Jon Thompson, Jono Tosch, Eric Trethewey, Dara Wier, Elizabeth Willis, and Mike Young.

This book was set in Apollo MT and Agency FB by the Center for Literary Publishing at Colorado State University. Copyedited by Joanna Doxey, proofread by Lincoln Greenhaw, and designed & typeset by Stephanie G'Schwind.